YOUR KNOWLEDGE HAS VALUE

AF151432

- We will publish your bachelor's and
  master's thesis, essays and papers

- Your own eBook and book -
  sold worldwide in all relevant shops

- Earn money with each sale

Upload your text at www.GRIN.com
and publish for free

Anders Alkærsig

The American Race Issue: Literacy as a Means to Freedom

GRIN Verlag

Bibliografische Information der Deutschen Nationalbibliothek:

Die Deutsche Bibliothek verzeichnet diese Publikation in der Deutschen National-
bibliografie; detaillierte bibliografische Daten sind im Internet über http://dnb.d-
nb.de/ abrufbar.

Imprint:

Copyright © 2011 GRIN Verlag GmbH
Druck und Bindung: Books on Demand GmbH, Norderstedt Germany
ISBN: 978-3-656-33981-6

This book at GRIN:

http://www.grin.com/en/e-book/206589/the-american-race-issue-literacy-as-a-means-
to-freedom

GRIN - Your knowledge has value

Der GRIN Verlag publiziert seit 1998 wissenschaftliche Arbeiten von Studenten, Hochschullehrern und anderen Akademikern als eBook und gedrucktes Buch. Die Verlagswebsite www.grin.com ist die ideale Plattform zur Veröffentlichung von Hausarbeiten, Abschlussarbeiten, wissenschaftlichen Aufsätzen, Dissertationen und Fachbüchern.

Visit us on the internet:

http://www.grin.com/

http://www.facebook.com/grincom

http://www.twitter.com/grin_com

The American Race Issue: Literacy as a Means to Freedom.

The subject of 'race throughout American history' has evolved around has evolved around and run up against innumerable variables. One could choose, for example, to investigate the race issue's relationship to labor market developments or any other equally important topic. However, due to the nature of the course, *American History and Literature*, of which this paper marks the ending, it is a natural consequence that this paper seeks to enquire into the race issue from a literary perspective. Again, hundreds of possible approaches present themselves to describe how the race issue has permeated literary history from the adoption of The Declaration of Independence in 1776 until now. This paper will approach literature's role in the race issue from two primary perspectives, namely that of Frederick Douglass' slave narrative in his *Narrative of the Life of Frederick Douglass, an American Slave*, and from that of Herman Melville's novella *Benito Cereno*. Rather than an actual textual analysis of the two authors' works, this paper will use them as tools to provide a glimpse of the nature of the race issue and to show how, in Frederick Douglass' case for instance, literacy does not equal freedom. The paper will attempt to investigate two separate perspectives of the race issue, namely, to present the living conditions of slaves as well as of liberated slaves in the 19th century through the works of, primarily, Frederick Douglass, but also Harriet Jacobs and to explore the racist mind of the white man through Herman Melville's *Benito Cereno*.

   The initial purpose of Frederick Douglass' slavery narrative was to "create a common bond between reader and narrator"[1] so, in other words, it was a tool for abolitionists to reveal slavery's brutal and cruel essence. Whilst still maintaining its initial purpose, the slave narrative evolved to be much more than a strictly autobiographical work. Though preserving an often-similar format, it crossed the boundary between autobiography and fiction. Frederick Douglass' *Narrative of the Life of Frederick Douglass, an American Slave* became one of the most prominent and widely read slave narratives and could arguably be considered the model for all subsequent slave narratives. A very basic, yet

---

[1] Lecater, page 15

utterly important and commonly questioned feature of Frederick Douglass' work is the fact that, rather than it being dictated to an editor, it was almost entirely written by Douglass himself. Frederick Douglass' authorship and its credibility underwent several attacks and though he initially was accused of "not look[ing], act[ing], think[ing], or speak[ing] like a man who had just recently escaped slavery"[2], a man who had known him while he was still named Frederick Bailey, though not then recognizing the intelligence present in his works, had thus known Frederick Douglass when he was still a bondsman and thereby confirmed Douglass' background.

The resentment vehemently expressed by Frederick Douglass when he was accused of forging the writing part of his authorship was not only a testament to how much he valued his literacy, but also showed his determination to prove that intelligence was not a matter of race, but a matter of upbringing and education. Continuing with this thought, fellow slave narrator Harriet Jacobs responded to "the underlying presumption that the Negro servant, or slave, was of a special inferior status"[3] by admitting "that the black man is inferior"; however, questioning the presumed fact that the gospels had the explanation for this inferiority she then asked: "what is it that makes it so? It is the ignorance in which white men compel him to live".[4]. Frederick Douglass' master stated that "a nigger should know nothing but to obey his master – to do as he is told to do. Learning would spoil the best nigger in the world... If you teach that nigger how to read, there would be no keeping him. It would forever unfit him to be a slave".[5] Such a statement shows, besides the harsh tone, that the slave masters were very aware of the fact that the proof of the black man's intelligence, namely his ability to read and write, could potentially lead to a demand for equality and, as a consequence of this equality, it could lead to a demand for freedom. The natural consequence of this realization was the law that forbade teaching slaves to read.

The slave, Frederick Douglass, actually escaped from captivity in the South. From then onwards his literacy was no longer the tool with which to

---

[2] Douglass, page 19
[3] Gross and Hardy, page 29
[4] Jacobs, page 39
[5] Douglass, page 78

achieve freedom: it had become, rather, the symbol of his freedom and independence. In *The Slave's Narrative* by Charles T. Davis and Henry Louis Gates Jr. this new purpose of his literacy is described as:

> The ability to utter his name, and more significantly to utter it in the mysterious characters on a page where it will continue to sound in silence so long as readers continue to construe the characters is what Douglass' *Narrative* is about, for in that lettered utterance is an assertion of identity, and in identity is freedom – freedom from slavery, freedom from ignorance, freedom from non-being, freedom even from time.[6]

The extract above not only shows how far former slaves such as Frederick Douglass had come and how far distant they had removed themselves from their past lives, it also firmly shows that literacy served as a skill that had the potential to help those slaves who were still in bondage and, thereby, it was an invaluable tool to the abolitionist cause.

Though there is no longer any doubt about Frederick Douglass' writing capabilities, there is, however, valid reason to question the reliability of his accounts. Without in any way claiming that slaves did not endure brutality and cruel living conditions, one can argue that either Frederick Douglass himself, an editor or his publisher could benefit greatly economically or politically from a narrative with a fitting description for their agenda of the life of a slave. An emphasis on brutality, inequality and injustice could not only function as a great argument against the pro-slavery supporters who still existed in the North, but the emphasis also made the text more attractive to a broader, action-craving, audience. Frederick Douglass addresses this very issue of reliability and relates to the great responsibility that producers of slave narratives have, the responsibility to represent their peers as well as the slaves still in bondage: "[we are] readers and self-conscious producers of narratives that were intended as literary works of art – as autobiographical acts performed as much in the service

---

[6] Davis and Gates, page 157

of literary posterity as on behalf of a contemporary mass of enslaved Afro-Americans".[7]

With statements such as the above, Frederick Douglass showed that he was well aware of the inherent pitfalls of his own literature and, by and large, he won the public over with the first version of *Narrative of the Life of Frederick Douglass, an American Slave*. Some debacles, however, arose when Frederick Douglass published *My Bondage and My Freedom* in 1855 and, in 1881 (and 1892), published *Life and Times of Frederick Douglass*. Frederick Douglass' first work had had strong abolitionist influence and had portrayed him as a young and intelligent slave who not only refused to accept his living conditions, but also escaped against all odds. The later works, however, received some criticism from the abolitionist quarter, because the revised narratives showed a somewhat more nuanced picture. With the general rule that in order for a former slave to be able to publish his works he had to have the backing of an abolitionist editor, it was extremely difficult for a former slave to impose his wishes if they differed from those of the editor, for a given work and thus "...the narrative lives of the ex-slaves were as much possessed by the abolitionists as their actual lives had been by the slaveholders".[8]

Even when relocated to the North, the former slaves had to endure the ever-present racism, which though nowhere near as bad as the brutal and cruel ways of the South, still very much existed. On page 138 of Harriet Jacobs' *Incidents in the Life of a Slave Girl*, she describes how she was refused service on a steamboat while her white colleagues were waited on properly. In addition, Harriet Jacobs later fled to Massachusetts where she hoped to escape the harsh and increasing racial terrorism against black people, a racism that to some extent obviously still existed throughout the 20th century in the United States of America. Frederick Douglass also encountered a society of the North that was permeated with racism, he found that "such was the strength of prejudice against color, among the white calkers [sic], that they refused to work with me and of course I could get no employment".[9] So, while Frederick Douglass and his peers

---

[7] Douglass, page 15
[8] Davis and Gates, page 154
[9] Douglass, page 150

had escaped slavery and bondage, they were still faced with a society with inherent prejudice and limited freedom for black people.

A key aspect that needs mention is the fact that even though slaves were freed from the bondage of slavery in the South, they were *purchased* free. In Frederick Douglass' case by a British couple and in Harriet Jacobs' case by a 'Mrs. Bruce'. The Fugitive Slave Bill meant that even though a slave escaped from South to North, he or she was still legally a slave until they were bought free. Alas, even though in Harriet Jacobs' case, she was bought to be free for the rest of her life, this freedom was rather tainted since Harriet Jacobs had a sense of "Love, duty, [and] gratitude"[10] she also felt that Mrs. Bruce "bind me to her side. It is a privilege to serve her who pities my oppressed people…"[11] So, despite that she is free, she still feels obliged to serve.

It is beyond doubt that Frederick Douglass and his fellow literate slaves' literacy played a vital role in the process of their escapes. Harriet Jacobs and Frederick Douglass were among the most important personalities in the abolitionist movement and their literacy is one of the most important reasons, if not the only one, for their role in the movement. The literate ex-slaves' role was to plant a seed of hope for the slaves who were still in bondage, to raise awareness among whites in the North of the brutality, injustice and cruelty in the South and to prove that intelligence is not dependent on race. For the abolitionists of the North, more specifically the abolitionist editors and publishers, the slaves needed to fit into the predominant stereotype of the slave narrative structure. What the literate slaves, de facto, did achieve was a technical freedom, but at the price of being indebted to their liberators.

Possibly due to its intriguing plot and the way in which it effectively addresses the issues of slavery and racism in America, Herman Melville's *Benito Cereno* is widely recognized as one of the most important works of the American antebellum era. *Benito Cereno* has, however, been accused of being a racist book or, at least, a book that acquiesces to the prevailing racial attitudes of its time. The method with which Herman Melville differentiates between the characters' opinions and his own narrator's opinion can easily lead to plausible

---

[10] Jacobs, page 156
[11] Jacobs, page 156

misunderstandings. Herman Melville uses cunning shifts between his authorial voice and that of Captain Delano, not only to make the story seem at first more plausible but also to make Delano's racist attitude apparent. Interestingly, it is also only through the subtle narrator's omniscient comments that one can discern Herman Melville's anti-slavery message.

One of the reasons why one *can* mistake *Benito Cereno* for a racist piece of literature is because there *is* racism in the book. Black people are constantly portrayed as inferior to whites. For instance, on board *San Dominick* they are described as "negro slaves, amongst other valuable freight"[12] thereby equating black slaves with mere cargo. The fact that Captain Delano is from abolitionist New England while still holding his racist views is a way for Herman Melville to show that even in the abolitionist North some people were, if not racists, then hypocrites. The fact that when seizing *San Dominick* the American sailors were motivated by potentially gaining its 'cargo' shows that even people of the abolitionist North still scorned black people: "to kill or maim the negroes was not the object. To take them, with the ship, was the object".[13]

The issue of the abolitionist North's hypocrisy is most apparent in two situations – firstly when Captain Delano describes his sympathy towards "negroes, not philanthropically, but genially, just as other men to Newfoundland dogs"[14] and, secondly, when he describes how black people are perfect for servile tasks:

> There is something in the Negro which, in a peculiar way, fits him for avocations about one's person. Most Negroes are natural valets and hair-dressers; taking to the comb and brush congenially as to the castanets [...]. And above all is the great gift of good-humor. Not the mere grin or laugh is here meant. Those were unsuitable. But a certain easy cheerfulness, harmonious in every glance and gesture; as though God had set the whole Negro to some pleasant tune.[15]

---

[12] Melville, page 36
[13] Melville, page 87
[14] Melville, page 71
[15] Melville, page 70

These two instances of racial prejudice show that Captain Delano, in some ways, has a 'well-meant' racist attitude. Unlike the crew of the *San Dominick,* he does not view the black slaves with hatred and inherent ferociousness. He does, on the other hand, view them with condescension and is undoubtedly patronizing in his observations. These two attitudes towards black people, the brutal one of the sailors and the more pitiful one of Captain Delano, could be viewed as Herman Melville's way of portraying the different kinds of racism in the North and in the South. The South has slavery and all the brutality and cruelty contained within it, whereas the North does not have slavery but is guilty of inequality and injustice in many other aspects of society and life – for example, the stereotyping of black people as being particularly fit for servants' jobs or the, at the time almost universally accepted, view that black people were intellectually inferior to white people.

As mentioned before, it is of utmost importance to pay careful attention to the narrative perspective of *Benito Cereno.* Failing to do so is the biggest obstacle to properly understanding the true meaning of the novella. Though it can be hard to distinguish between Captain Delano's voice and the omniscient narrator's voice, we learn, explicitly, that Captain Delano has a questionable reliability:

> [Delano is] a person of a singularly undistrustful good nature, not liable, except on extraordinary and repeated incentives, and hardly then, to indulge in personal alarms, any way involving the imputation of malign evil in man. Whether, in view of what humanity is capable, such a trait implies, along with a benevolent heart, more than ordinary quickness and accuracy of intellectual perception, may be left to the wise to determine.[16]

Though the above does function as a declaration of Captain Delano's unreliability, Herman Melville quickly rejects it again by stating that "whatever misgivings might have obtruded on first seeing the stranger, would almost, in

---

[16] Melville, page 35

any seaman's mind, have been dissipated by observing that, the ship, in navigating into the harbor, was drawing too near the land".[17] By following this chain of thoughts from Captain Delano, Herman Melville, through the voice of the narrator, makes it possible for the reader to maintain the dual perspective of the story – he does not, for the purpose of the story, discredit Captain Delano's viewpoints too much, too soon. On many occasions Herman Melville chooses to strengthen Captain Delano's reliability and thus, by almost omitting the omniscient narrator's voice, the reader is interpreting the novella under the condition of Captain Delano's viewpoint. Even in these instances, there are, however, clues that suggest questioning Captain Delano's attitude. In Captain Delano's chain of thoughts there are many things that 'seem' or 'appear', whereas nothing seems to be certain or definitive.

One, some might say, obvious perspective is missing in *Benito Cereno*, namely that of the black slaves. This lack of perspective serves the notion of a very one-sided concept of justice. While *Benito Cereno* does not function as a complete and adequate account of the events during the revolt it does, however, comment, with descriptions of the 'innocent'[18] white man, the prevailing racial attitude among American whites in the 19th century. One might be on thin ice to assume Herman Melville purposely designed *Benito Cereno* to be misunderstood, but these understandable misunderstandings forced the reader, with the same shortcomings they potentially had in common with Captain Delano, to confront their attitudes. The implications of a blindsided approach to *Benito Cereno* and an exploration of the white racist attitudes will be explored in the following part.

As mentioned before, Captain Delano reveals his views about black people on numerous occasions. He does not see them as real people, more like "Newfoundland dogs",[19] and his mention of black people's supposed genetic limitations and the fact that he thinks they are "too stupid"[20] show that he does not see humanity in black people. On several occasions Herman Melville makes Captain Delano's inadequacies apparent and thus he shows, through his

---

[17] Melville, page 35
[18] Melville, page 101
[19] Melville, page 71
[20] Melville, page 63

omniscient narrator's comments, his own opinion: namely that the allegation that black people are genetically inferior to white people cannot be upheld. Furthermore, Herman Melville shows, through the description of Babo, that black people are, in fact, capable of the exact same things as any others. Babo is described as a "hive of subtlety"[21] and he "had schemed and led the revolt".[22] Babo's clever planning and execution of the revolt is in sharp contrast with Captain Delano's failure to recognize Babo's capabilities as a leader.

Since *Benito Cereno* was published in 1855 it has been criticized for supporting the pro-slavery and racist cause. However, by examining the text with extreme vigilance for the presence of the subtle narrator, one can prove this assertion wrong. While it is true that the black people in the novella act violently in their revolt, the supposition that Herman Melville had the intent of showing black people as made of pure evil can be proven wrong. Herman Melville shows how white people and black people are equally violent by, for instance, describing how Babo's head is cut off and how the Spanish sailors attack the chained slaves. In describing the violence committed by both the white and the black people, Herman Melville shows how he views the relationship between the races. There are more similarities than differences. Furthermore, he portrays the black slaves as people with a goal. They are not motiveless in their violence. They are violent and order the murder of Aranda so as to "be sure of their liberty"[23] and one can argue that, if Babo is evil, he is only evil because he fights evil and injustice. It can consequently be stated that Herman Melville, through his omniscient narrator, seeks to establish the notion that races should not be divided along the lines of good and evil, and simultaneously also questions whether violence is an appropriate means to attain freedom.

Through Captain Delano's conscious, we can use *Benito Cereno* to explore the white racist mind. By carefully separating Captain Delano's view from that of the omniscient narrator one discovers that Captain Delano to a great extent feels satisfaction in his "...weakness for negroes"[24] and his sentiments

---

[21] Melville, page 102
[22] Melville, page 102
[23] Melville, page 92
[24] Melville, page 71

toward black people are "like [those of] most men of a good, blithe heart".[25] By describing the "...indisputable inferior..."[26] black people and their "docility arising from the unaspiring contentment of a limited mind",[27] Captain Delano appears almost humorously hypocritical and without the slightest bit of self-knowledge. It is as if he is, unknowingly, describing himself.

One can, bearing in mind the previous observations, arguably state that most of the questions regarding racial attitude in *Benito Cereno* can be answered with this simple statement: the portrayal of blacks in *Benito Cereno* is balanced. Throughout the story Herman Melville describes the blacks as humanly as possible; he describes how their violent acts are adequately motivated and, thus, waives any assertion of their excessive malignity. Herman Melville shows on several occasions how blacks and whites are equally intelligent and, furthermore, he highlights the whites' deficient knowledge of it. The message of the story, however, is not easily understood. It demands substantial effort to realize what the true message of the novella and, so, it may be hard for Herman Melville's contemporary readership to understand.

One question, nonetheless, is left unanswered: whether it is wrong or right to fight the war between good and evil with violence such as the revolt depicted. Herman Melville uses the brutal and appalling portrayal of the righteous revolt to raise this question. The question is left unanswered but the mere dramatization of the revolt makes the black man's voice heard.

This paper has focused on two quite different pieces of literature and tried to put them into a historical context. Frederick Douglass' slave narrative has, from a former slave's viewpoint, describes the impact of the slave issue, both in the North and in the South, whereas Herman Melville's *Benito Cereno* has undergone an investigation primarily focused on the white man's racial attitude and the hypocrisy it contains. It is safe to say that much of the progress that was made in the 19th century, in regard of the race issue, did not lead to immediate freedom, equality or justice. They did, however, pave the way for the progress we have seen in the 20th century.

---

[25] Melville, page 71
[26] Melville, page 71
[27] Melville, page 71

Bibliography

Davis, C. and Gates, Jr, H. L. (eds). 1985. *The Slave's Narrative*. New York: Oxford University Press.

Douglass, F. 1986. *Narrative of the Life of Frederick Douglass, an American Slave*. New York: Penguin.

Gross, S. and Hardy, J. 1966. *Images of the Negro in American Literature*. Chicago: University of Chicago Press.

Jacobs, H. 2001. *Incidents in the Life of a Slave Girl*. Edited by N. McKay and F. Smith Foster. New York: Norton.

Lecater Bland Jr, S. 2000. *Voices of the Fugitives: Runaway Slave Stories and their Fictions of Self-Creation*. Connecticut: Praeger.

Melville, Herman. 2002. *Benito Cereno*. In *Melville's Short Novels. Authorative Texts, Contexts, Criticism*, edited by Dan McCall, 34-102. New York, London: W. W. Norton & Company, Inc.